PRAYER EVOLVING

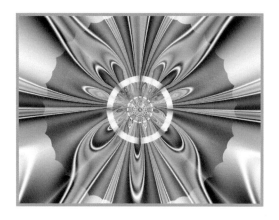

PRAYER EVOLVING

FIVE PERSONAL EXPLORATIONS
INTO THE FUTURE OF PRAYER

DENNIS RIVERS

FEATURING THE FRACTAL PAINTINGS OF
VICKY BRAGO-MITCHELL

KARUNA BOOKS

BERKELEY, CALIFORNIA, USA

Prayer Evolving

by Dennis Rivers

ISBN: 9780966990898

Cover and title page illustrations:
Front cover: Starstorm -- Back cover: Tesoro -- Title page: Transformation
Fractal paintings by Vicky Brago-Mitchell – Used with the artist's permission.

Karuna Books – www.KarunaBooks.net
is an imprint of **Human Development Books**
1563 Solano Ave. #164 -- Berkeley, California, 94707 -- USA
This book can be ordered through local and online bookstores around
the world. To find one near you, please visit www.HuDevBooks.com

All books and essays published by Karuna Books
are available free of charge in PDF format at our
web site: www. KarunaBooks.net

TABLE OF CONTENTS

PRAYER EVOLVING
FIVE PERSONAL EXPLORATIONS
INTO THE FUTURE OF PRAYER

TABLE OF CONTENTS

ABOUT THE ILLUSTRATIONS AND ILLUSTRATORS

A bow of deepest gratitude to Vicky Brago-Mitchell, who graciously allowed me to use her artwork in this book. All of the illustrations of hers that you find here are available as prints from her art gallery at Karuna Books: www.karunabooks.net/visionary-art/. Deep thanks also to the many other artists whose works illuminate this book. You can find links to many of their web sites at the link mentioned above. Over the many years of its writing, great effort has been made to secure permission to reproduce the artwork that appears in this book-available-to-everyone, but in some cases I was not able to locate the artist. If some artwork of yours appears in this book without your permission and you would like to arrange formal permission (or request that a particular item be removed), please contact me at rivers@newconversations.net.

CHAPTER ONE

PRAYERS WITHIN THE HEART OF GOD

INTRODUCTION

Over the course of my lifetime, I have been moved by a deep spiritual restlessness to press forward into the unknown territory of new forms of prayer. This book is record of my explorations.

For a period of about ten years, from 1963 to 1973, I engaged in intensive practice of rote forms of prayer, repeating many hours a day words of prayer exactly as they had been taught to me. But at some point in that process I had a crisis of faith. What need had God of a living tape recorder, playing, as it were, on an endless loop? How much real love was there in my prayers? What was my relationship with the Ground of Being with whom I was trying to have a conversation? What creative processes might allow me to be more fully present in that conversation? This book is the record of my searching inside of myself to find answers to these kinds of questions.

In this first chapter on visual imagery and creativity in the life of prayer, I explore the theme of being *inside* of the being of God, sometimes expressed as the infinitely beautiful, infinitely loving Heart of God and sometimes expressed as the infinitely luminous Mind of God.

Our usual way of thinking about God, as a separate being, often implies the very separation we hope to overcome. While I still sometimes pray to God as a separate being, I have also, over the past ten years, begun to explore acknowledging God as the source of my being, life of my life and breath of my breath, and the source of all my experience of self-giving love. (...and thus, for me, often too near to be addressed as a separate person.) Through these visual prayers I seek to live in a closer communion with the inner presence of God, understood as Infinite Love, Energy, Awareness and Understanding.

In searching for ways to open myself more deeply to this Presence, I have incorporated into my life of prayer the most vivid imagery I can possibly imagine. While some people might question the role of imagination in the life of prayer, I have become convinced over the course of years of meditation and prayer that imagination actually plays a crucial role in both spiritual and everyday life. If I "can't imagine" something happening, I probably will not let it happen. It is by repeatedly imagining myself as an electrician or pilot or writer, that I mobilize my inner resources to become one. And, I believe, it is by repeatedly imagining my capacity to be filled with infinite love that I make a place for that beautiful energy to come into my heart. Imagination is not all that is required, just as one might say that the heart is not the only organ in the human body. But just as heart plays a central role in the functioning of the body, so I believe our capacity to imagine plays a central role in our spiritual lives. "Without a vision," the Soul of the Universe proclaims in the Hebrew Bible, "my people perish."

Having made this strong affirmation about imagery and imagination in the life of prayer, I would also like to affirm the place of silence, of quiet openness. I take the alternating of in-breath and out-breath, and the cycles of the tides and seasons, as models for everything in life. Thus, I am convinced that the effortful practices that I describe in these essays are most fruitful when they are practiced in an alternating cycle with periods of deep, restful silence. When you plant a seed of something deep and beautiful in your mind, your mind needs time to grow a response to it.

I invite you to explore these four prayers and to adapt them to fit your own spiritual life and your own relationship to the Divine, be that through Jesus, Allah, Buddhamind, Krishna, YHWH, Mary, Milky Way, Infinite Mother, Spirits of the Grandfathers and Grandmothers, or through one of the many other "Windows of the Divine" (which, due to limits of space and the limits of my own knowledge, I do not list here). At the end of the four prayers listed below, you will find a brief essay describing in more detail how I became inspired to write them.

May infinite kindness shine forth in each of our lives. And may we each find the strength to work for a world full kindness, forgiveness and cooperation.

Dennis Rivers, 1993
(revised 2007)

Starstorm   Fractal painting by Vicky Brago-Mitchell

1. INDWELLING

The seed of the Spiral:

> I am in the loving heart of God
> wide as the morning sky
> I am in the radiant heart of Being
> fragrant as a flowering tree
> I am in the loving heart of the Universe
> shining with endless Light
> I am in the infinite heart of God
> Whose presence caresses me like a warm wind
> I am in the loving heart of Being
> which sings through me with angelic voices
> I am in the endless heart of the Universe
> who holds me like a sleeping child

The Spiral deepens:

I am in the loving heart of God
    wide as the morning sky and full of golden light
    that fills the entire horizon of my life.
    As I walk deeper and deeper into that light
    I become filled with a deep peace.

I am in the radiant heart of Being
    fragrant as a flowering tree.
    I press my face into the blossoming branches
    and my body fills up and overflows
    with the perfume of compassion and delight.

I am in the loving heart of the Universe
    shining with endless Light
    I feel the warmth of this endless Light
    washing through me with each breath

I am in the infinite heart of God
    which caresses me like a warm wind
    the hands of the wind are full of joyous electricity
    which fills me to overflowing

I am in the loving heart of Being
    full of angelic voices, singing,
    I hear them, first far away,
    then closer, then all around me,
    then deep within me.
    As their voices become clearer
    I realize they are announcing
    infinite forgiveness.
    As their voices become clearer
    I realize their voices are my own.

I am in the endless heart of the Universe
    who holds me like a newborn child
    and rocks me to sleep
    on the front porch of eternity.
    Every time I go to sleep
    I go to sleep deep within
    the endlessly loving,
    endlessly beautiful heart of God.

2. BECOMING THE LIGHT:
A MEDITATION WITHIN THE LUMINOUS MIND OF GOD

I am in the luminous Mind of God
which opens before me like endless fields of flowers
rippling gently in a fragrant wind
over rolling hills in waves of color
glowing in a sparkling light
that seems to come from everywhere.
I look down at my body and see
that I too am glowing with light.
Everything becomes clearer and clearer and clearer
and I experience all that is muddled in me
becoming clearer, too.

The loving light that is the Mind of God
is shining in me and through me and
filling me with compassion for everyone,
myself included!
It is slowly filling me up
like a mysterious liquid light.
As it fills me more and more completely
I start to smile... it has reached my heart.

My hands begin to glow and now I feel as if
the light is filling up the space behind my eyes.
When the light has filled me up to the top of my head
I feel it overflowing out of me
into the space around me.
I feel currents of endless forgiveness
flowing through me, filling me with enormous power.
I am radiant now, shining like the Sun,
radiating light of compassion in every direction
and full of energy.
Everything and everyone I may have feared or hated,
I can now face.
Everything and everyone I may have feared or hated,
I can now see with the light of forgiveness.
Everything and everyone I may have feared or hated,
I can now bless
to be transformed by that Light.

Fractal painting by Vicky Brago-Mitchell

3. BECOMING THE LIGHT TOGETHER:
   A MEDITATION OF TWO OR MORE
   WITHIN THE LUMINOUS MIND OF GOD

We stand together, facing one another
within the luminous Mind of God
which opens before us
like endless fields of flowers
rippling gently in a fragrant wind
over rolling hills in waves of color
glowing in a sparkling light
that seems to come from everywhere.
I look at your face and I realize
that we are both glowing with light.
Everything becomes clearer and clearer
 and clearer,
our souls join hands,
and we experience all that was confused in us
becoming clearer, too.

The loving light in the Mind of God
is shining in us and through us and
filling us with compassion for everyone,
ourselves included.
It is slowly filling us up
like a mysterious liquid light
as it fills us more and more completely
we start to smile... it has reached our hearts.
Our hands begin to glow
and as we look into each other's eyes
our faces get brighter and brighter.

When the light
has filled us up to the top of our heads
we feel it overflowing out of us

into the space around us
we feel currents of endless forgiveness
flowing through us
filling us with enormous power.

We are radiant now, shining like the Sun,
radiating light in every direction
and full of energy.
Everything and everyone
we may have feared or hated,
we can now face.
Everything and everyone
we may have feared or hated,
we can now see with the light of forgiveness.
Everything and everyone
we may have feared or hated,
we can now bless
to be transformed by that Light.

Tesoro   Fractal painting by Vicky Brago-Mitchell

4. TRANSFORMATION

I am in the loving Mind of the Milky Way
that sings through every cell of my body
with millions of angelic voices
filling me with energy and courage
to enter more deeply into the healing
of all that is wounded
in myself and in the world around me.
I am in the Beautiful Energy of God
which washes through me
with a trillion singing sparkles
washing away all my confusion
and filling me with light...
washing away all my grudges
and filling my heart with the fragrance of flowers.
Anyone who may ever have wronged me,
I release into the light of God.
Anyone who may ever have abused me,
I release into the light of God.
Anyone who may ever have hated me,
I release into the light of God and bless to be healed in all ways.
In my minds eye they grow smaller and smaller
as I let them go... let them go... let them go...
into the endless light of God's healing love.
The beautiful energy of God's healing love,
warm as a mother holding her newborn
is filling the space where I used to carry them.
A deep sense of gratitude
for all the blessings of today, the sun, the sky,
the earth beneath my feet,
for every act of kindness, anywhere,
is filling the space where I used to carry my resentments
and I open my life to be a window
through which new blessings can pour into the world.

Transformation   Fractal painting by Vicky Brago-Mitchell

As I open myself to be a window of blessing
the beautiful energy of God washes me
more and more deeply.
Everyone I have ever hated or resented
I release into the light of God,
asking for forgiveness
and opening myself to be forgiven.
Everyone I have ever injured or abused
I release into the light of God,
asking for forgiveness and
opening myself to be forgiven.
The light surrounds me
and I experience a forgiveness
that expands in all directions.
I forgive them, they forgive me,
and the infinitely beautiful heart of God
forgives us all, setting us free.

5. AUTOBIOGRAPHICAL NOTES ON
PRAYERS WITHIN THE HEART OF GOD [1995]

INTRODUCTION

I first became interested in the spiritual life more than forty years ago when I was a teenager, and have been practicing one or another forms of prayer and meditation ever since. Some time around the year 1990 I experienced an abrupt change in my relationship to that larger, mysterious source of life to Whom we pray. It was a shift from feeling "outside" of the being of God to feeling "inside," and it is the most important thing that has ever happened to me, although I can't express the significance of the change nearly as well as I would like to.

Around the time of that change I happen to have been studying the new psychology of visualization, and so it occurred to me to try to express this new attitude in vivid imagery. In the pages that follow I would like to both share the history of my explorations with you and encourage you to explore vivid positive imagery in your own prayer life. These notes mix together autobiography and spiritual philosophy, confession and reflection, because that is just how these prayers came to be. They evolved out of the interplay of my meditation, my struggles toward love and awareness, and my efforts to understand what various saints, mystics and psychologists have thought and taught about the spiritual life.

It is important for me to state that I do not possess, so far as I know, any special spiritual gifts. Actually, I believe that love is the greatest spiritual gift of all, and we all possess the capacity to love in infinite measure, no matter how much or how little we have developed it. My experiments are the experiments of an ordinary human being, therefore I hope that any other human being will be able to perform similar experiments, if so inclined. We are all, as I see it, "authorized by the Universe" to be more creative, more compassionate and more understanding. Everything I write is written with "it seems to me" in mind (only it gets tiresome to put that in each sentence) and I hope that you will explore what rings true for you and leave aside what does not.

My hope in sharing this part of my spiritual journey with you is not that you will agree with everything I say, but rather that you may be encouraged to enter more deeply and more enthusiastically into your own unique inner life. I hope this material will encourage you to express more fully the unique prayer that is hidden your own heart, and in doing so to find your own unique way of opening more fully to the Greater Life that breathes through us all.

AUTOBIOGRAPHY

I was born in 1941, the child of a Jewish mother and a Catholic father who had become a student of Tibetan Buddhism. The strongest memories of my childhood in Los Angeles are of my father's many mysterious books, of going to various churches and temples, and of the weekly air raid drills at school in which my grammar school classmates and I prepared to (supposedly) live through an atom bomb blast.

I was a very introspective kid, inspired by my father's search for an inner light and uncertain about my prospects in a world full of violence. As a child I discovered that there was no particular building where I belonged on Sunday mornings, and no particular set of prayers that were meant for me. By the time I was a teenager I knew that I would have to find my own spiritual way. By the time I was in my early twenties, I was exploring the life of continuous prayer and meditation as a disciple of a Sikh mystical teacher.

My years in the meditation community were followed by years in the Vietnam war, years living on mountain tops, years studying comparative religion and theology, years of protest, and years coping with the assassination of my heroes.

As I look back on my life I see that my entire life has been framed by the threat of violence on one side and the promise of an inner light on the other, an unsettling and incomprehensible contrast. It is only recently that I have come to see that these are the two sides of the couplets in the Prayer of St. Francis: "Where there is injury, may I sow forgiveness, where there is hatred, may I sow love," etc.

The Prayer of St. Francis suggests that we continually walk through life with troubles in one hand and love in the other. Our life assignment seems to be to bring the love into the middle of the troubles.

AGREEMENT ON THE QUALITIES OF GOD

Although religious people argue about God all the time, there is actually a wonderful agreement among most world religions that the Being of the Greater Life includes a kind of trinity. The first element of this trinity is infinite love, the second is infinite awareness, intelligence and understanding and the third is infinite, life-giving, life-sustaining and life-healing power or energy. From this "shared faith" perspective, it is these beautiful qualities of the Divine Life that are the deep common ground of our spiritual quests, not the labels and images people use to remind themselves about those qualities. Mystics of many faiths, including Navajo, Sufi, Hindu, and Christian, report the experience that all these qualities combine into a single overwhelming beauty.

Because we all have different temperaments and different backgrounds, we will almost certainly need to use different labels to remind ourselves to turn toward that beauty. My experience has also been that these labels and reminders will change over the course of a person's lifetime. An important step in the deepening of my inner life was to begin searching for the unique images in my own life experience that actually reminded me of these qualities. In these pages I use many different images of the Greater Life: the Heart of God, Mind of God, Energy of God, the Source, the Mother of the Universe, etc. As you read the prayer explorations please feel free to substitute any image that reminds YOU of infinite love, wisdom and/or energy, either singly or all together.

Many spiritual traditions also agree that the goal of the spiritual life is to be a kind of window or channel through which these qualities of the Divine Life can pour into the world, transforming us and the world at the same time. The prayers presented here, which are all on the opening-to-the-infinite theme, express this understanding of the spiritual life.

I am in the loving heart of God,
as bright as the Sun,
blazing with a million colors

VISUALIZATION

My first introduction to the topic of visualization was a mimeographed manifesto, with pages of various colors, that I ordered around 1960 from an advertisement in the back pages of *Fate Magazine* (a source of information, at mid-century, about all things spiritual and paranormal). At that time the topic of visualization was on the fringes of American culture, loosely associated with mental healing. The author of the manifesto, Clarence Van Vredenberg, advocated visualizing with all one's senses, imagining smells and sounds and textures as well as scenes. This, he wrote, would carry one's positive suggestions much deeper into one's creative mind, and guide a person to success in all things.

The past four decades have moved the topics of visualization and mental healing out of the "fringe" and into the mainstream of psychology. Hundreds, if not thousands, of books and articles have been written on the topic of visualization, and the subject of inner imagery has become an important focus of attention in both psychology and medicine. This interest in visualization and inner imagery has given rise to exuberant new schools of thought: neuro-linguistic programming, psycho-neuro-immunology, and archetypal psychology among them. There is a wide consensus among writers and researchers on the topic of visualization that multi-sensory 'visualizations' generally have deeper effects than the simple repetition of words (although even a single word can have a deep calming effect).

I am in the infinitely beautiful heart of God
who holds me in her arms
like a mother holding her newborn child

The "Prayers Within the Heart of God" experiment in prayer grew out of my effort to apply these ideas about vivid visualization to the deeper reaches of my inner life. Two kinds of experiences drew me in that direction.

EXPANDING THE GOAL OF VISUALIZATION

First, I was often frustrated by the narrow focus of the visualization exercises I studied. There were exercises for losing weight, to stop smoking, to feel better about oneself, etc. The focus of many exercises was the symptom of a problem. I kept on wondering: What about my whole life? My relationship to God, the Cosmos, the great Whatever-it-is in which we "live and move and have our being." I wanted something that would address the totality of my life.

It is true that traditions of visual prayer exist in many of the world's religions, Christianity, Hinduism and Buddhism included.

But traditional religions tend to have a one-size-fits-all approach. You stand in line and do what you are told. I was never very good at either of these. My previous efforts at blind obedience had ended in deep disappointment, and I didn't see my former companions in blind obedience getting anywhere either. I had tried very sincerely, often for years at a time, to do spiritual exercises from distant lands and distant times. It never worked all that well and left me feeling that I needed to pray with images that were closer to my own life.

I am in the luminous Mind of the Universe
which fills me with endless creative energy

LIVING WITH JOY AND SORROW

The second experience that drew me toward these experiments was a growing sense of my limits as a peace and ecology activist. The world I lived in was calling me to be a healing and reconciling influence.

It was and is a world full of extraordinary cruelty, greed and pain. Jesus said, "Whatsoever you do to the least of these, you do to me." By which I understand him to be saying, among other things, that we can't simultaneously open ourselves wide enough to let in a healing love and joy, and close ourselves off to the suffering of our sisters and brothers. But by the late 1980's I found myself nearing what seemed to be the limit of the sorrow I could carry.

I was concerned about several issues: peace, ecology, and human rights, none of which were getting better. The peace organization I was working for went through a crisis and imploded with bad feelings. When the four Jesuit priests, their house-keeper and her daughter were murdered in El Salvador, the last of my hope left me. There was no limit, it seemed, to how ugly it could get out there, and no safe place for peace-makers, either. Spiritually, I had run out of gas.

Over the next several years I gradually became aware that the deeper the ugliness and pain I intended to face, both in the world and inside of myself, the deeper the love and beauty I needed to find, to know, to center myself in. I needed my own mental and emotional "love-in" that I could carry around with me. Otherwise, I was simply going to be swallowed up by the tide of bad news. In the 1960s I experienced these two themes as irreconcilable opposites: facing pain of the world, on the one hand, and finding love and beauty, on the other. Now I see them deeply interwoven. The amount of suffering I am able to face now seems directly related to the quality of the love I have experienced, how joyous and self-giving it was and is. The amount of love I am able to experience, to let in, now seems to me to be directly related to a courageous openness that does not turn away from pain. Finally, to be a healing influence requires of me that I remember what it feels like to be happy, that I keep alive in myself a vision of mutual fulfillment and reconciliation. I am now convinced that my heart must somehow become large enough to hold both joy and sorrow. Only then, it seems to me, can my life be a bridge between the two.

We live, now and forever, infinitely embraced
in the radiant heart of Mary, Mother of God,
who melts away all that is wounded in us.

NEW IMAGES

The question of how one goes about opening oneself to the experience of a joyous and self-giving love is not a question to which any society has an easy answer. The same holds true for opening oneself to the experience of beauty, as a quick visit to most art galleries will attest. So in the beginning of my quest I was at a loss as to how to proceed, but the question itself filled me energy. How does one go about opening oneself to the experience of a joyous and self-giving love?

The literature on visualization suggests that our lives are deeply influenced by a set of images we carry around inside our heads. They come largely from our family history, our successes and failures, and from television, movies and advertising. This process of collecting one's set of inner images is often like throwing random ingredients into a pot and hoping they will turn into a good tasting soup. The images we have collected don't always fit together well or sustain us through difficult times. The good news is that we can change them.

These images appear to stay active in our brains through a process of unconscious repetition. In that lies one possible key to change. If repetition is what keeps the old images alive, we can choose to repeat something new, just the way we learn a new song and hum the melody to ourselves.

Encouraged by this vision of new possibilities I set out to create a new set of life affirming mental images. I drew from everything I had ever learned about the spiritual life and the most positive experiences I had ever had. Although I didn't remember it at the time (1990), at some point during the previous decade I had seen a television special on Mother Teresa, in which she had taught a new member of her order to pray, "I am in the heart of Jesus and Jesus is in my heart." Much later (1996) I realized that my *Prayers Within the Heart of*

God were and are an attempt to extend and universalize the spirit of that prayer.

INNER RESOURCES

Almost every human being has had some experiences of love, beauty and inner rightness that are beyond the boundaries of everyday life. Precisely because there is very little way to express these experiences in the ordinary story of a day's events, we lose touch with them. Unfortunately, we tend to remember our worst experiences quite vividly but lose track of our best moments(not completely forgotten, but rarely remembered). This sets the stage for us to repeat our worst experiences rather than our best. Once having developed a coherent story, people easily ignore events that are not consistent with it. The visual prayers became for me a way of cultivating a new story that has more openings for states of profound well being.

PRAYING AS-IF-ALREADY-RECEIVED

Among the teachings of Jesus there is one that I have always found both deeply inspiring and deeply puzzling. In The Gospel of Mark, Chapter 11, verse 24, Jesus tells his listeners "whatever you ask for in prayer, believe that you have received it, and it will be yours."

To be respectful of this verse, it is important to note that it is part of a complex lesson about faith, prayer and forgiveness. I don't think it can be understood without also remembering the "Thy will be done" emphasis in other parts of Jesus' prayer teaching. While there are many unresolved questions in my mind about praying for material objects or effects, the situation is much clearer for me regarding what might be called the gifts of the spirit. We need not only food and shelter and protection from earthquakes, we also need love, awareness, forgiveness, wisdom and many other gifts of the spirit. These may be available in infinite supply from a source we don't understand, if we will open ourselves to receive them in an infinite way. In relation to these inward gifts the "pray as if you have already received" principle may be as powerful as we are willing to let it be.

Perhaps one element at work here is this: if we can't imagine ourselves receiving a particular blessing, we may not be able to let in the blessing even if it is continuously pounding on our door, begging to be let in. So part of my asking needs to include the willingness to let go of my old picture of myself as "lacking" and develop a new picture of myself as "receiving" and "worthy of having." Since I grew up in a culture that is always in a hurry, it is tempting for me to want to change my image of myself from "lacking" to "receiving" in a single blazing moment. But my experience has been that the mind is like a garden and that a gentle gardening of the new images probably works better than a sudden revolution against the old ones.

I have very little to suggest concerning praying for healing or for material needs. If I were in a falling airplane, I don't know what I would do or pray. I hope I would have the presence of mind to pray any prayer at all (perhaps to give thanks for having been alive and for having participated in the great mystery of love). But it seems to me that such extreme crisis situations, which come to mind so easily, are not a fruitful model for trying to understand how to open ourselves to more blessings in everyday life.

Perhaps if we open ourselves to more love, more understanding and more life-sustaining energy and beauty, we can work together better to make sure that our own and everyone else's material needs are met. Perhaps if the mechanics' (and airline owners') hearts had been more full of love, they would have done a more careful job of maintaining the airplane. Recent research in which prayer groups focused on hospitals revealed that prayers on the open-ended theme of "Thy will be done" seemed to have more positive effect on the hospital patients than prayers for specific healing action.

I hope in time I will understand more of what is going on in such cases. For now I accept it as a wonderful mystery, what Joseph Chilton Pearce called a "crack in the cosmic egg," through which we glimpse a possibility that calls us to explore more deeply. For me, one possible implication of the teaching that "God is love" is that God's influence comes into the world primarily through love, rather than through the kind of mechanical force required to protect people from hail storms, keep sinking ships afloat, etc. It is not that I want to close the door on miracles. What I want is to open the door wider for the quiet miracle of love.

THE WAY OF INNER BLESSING

The deepest blessings I can imagine are also qualities of God: ever-expanding love, awareness, understanding and a healing, life-giving energy, all somehow woven together and each one enriching all the others.

Many mystics from religions as diverse as Hinduism and Catholicism would insist that rays of these qualities are raining down upon us (or yearning to be expressed from a source deep within us) at this very moment, and at every moment of every day! This is a recurring theme in the writings of many mystics, from Meister Eckhart to Ramakrishna. As I have struggled to understand these extraordinary assertions, I find that my emphasis in prayer has shifted away from asking God to give me these deeper blessings and shifted toward opening myself more fully to receive them.

There has been a progression in my prayers over the years, from "Oh God, please get me out of this painful mess," and "Oh God, please find me someone to love," to "Oh luminous Buddha-mind, please make me a kinder person," to the prayers the prayers in this chapter, which arose spontaneously in my mind as prayers from within the being of God, rather than being outside and asking for something.

Looking back now on the emergence of these prayers in my consciousness, I recognize in them the quality of "praying as if I have already received," about which I have been puzzling for a lifetime. We start out as young adults searching for love. It takes a while to realize that we can never receive enough affirmation to satisfy our deep unfulfilled need to give, to affirm, to embody. Whether we realize it or not, it seems to me that we are all on a journey to *become* more the love we hoped to receive.

I am in the loving Mind of the Milky Way
that sings through every cell of my body
with millions of angelic voices
and fills me with energy
to help with the healing
of all that is wounded
in the world around me

Mother Universe   NASA Photograph

6. POSTSCRIPT -- JULY 1998:
JOURNAL NOTES ON LETTING IN MORE LOVE

This morning I was thinking
about these prayers of reassurance
and wondering to what degree
all of this is artificial,
smoke and mirrors in the hallways of my mind.
What is going on when I reassure myself
that I am continually in the light of God's love, etc?
Then it struck me the with force of a revelation
that a large part of the feeling of being loved
is always a creative re-enactment!
Exactly as in early childhood development
(according to various "object relations" theorists):
when mother leaves the room
the two-year-olds fight off the terror of abandonment
by vividly visualizing mommy
and vocalizing mommy
and reminding themselves of mommy's hugs
by hugging their teddy bears.

In ordinary life, I think we undervalue
the role that *imagination* plays
in the process of becoming a mature person.
Out of that heroic visualizing of mommy
when mommy is not there
comes our capacity to imagine kindness
even though we live in a world soaked with cruelty,
to imagine justice in a world of oppression,
to imagine buildings as yet unbuilt,
and to nurture ourselves
through times of great isolation
with the memory love
and the knowledge that love is possible.

Therefore,
and this for me is an earth-shaking "therefore,"
the experience of being loved
can not be understood only in terms
of the objective facts about who actually loves us.

We have also to look
at how skillfully and creatively
we carry that love around with us.
How is it that we know we are loved
when the person who loves us
walks out of the room?
And as adults we know, at some level,
that everyone will die
and could die this very day in some sort of accident.
How is it that we are not immobilized
with the fear that those who love us and their love
will be taken away?
One possible answer, for me,
is that love is something like a candle flame:
it needs an external flame to get it going
but once on fire
it burns from its own inner fuel.
As an African-American teenager said once
of her inner-city mentor and friend,
"Sister Monica loves us
until we learn to love ourselves."

We need other people to love us, <u>and</u>...
we play a very large role
in the receiving of that love,
according to how we let the love in,
symbolize it, honor it, celebrate it, give thanks for it,
make it a permanent part of our life story,
allow it to be transformed into a healthy self-esteem,

and find ways of going back to it
as an emotional starting place, when we get lost.
Perhaps you feel yourself
resisting these suggestions.
I certainly do resist them!
For much of my life I've thought of love
as if it were water:
it's over there and I want some.
My experience of love had, I thought,
everything to do with that woman over there
or God or Jesus or my beloved guru, Charan Singh,
and not much to do with any activity on my part.
As a country song intoned in the 1980s:
"Kick me through the goal posts of life, Sweet Jesus!"
What a jolt to realize
that I am part of the process.

Photo by Randy Wang

No familiar ideas guide me on this road
of inner opening
hence my *Prayers Within the Heart of God*
excursions into the uncharted territory of gratitude.

Love is deeply interwoven
with the experience of gratefulness,
and perhaps understanding gratitude
can be a doorway into understanding love.
Everyday the sun shines upon the corn fields
so that I might eventually eat some enchiladas.

How much am I willing to let myself
feel the miracle of this?

Everyday the Earth gives me life
in a thousand ways, but I could say
well, it's just an ordinary day,
nothing new, same as yesterday.
How is it that have I set
my threshold of gratitude so high
that it sometimes seems
nothing short of winning a galactic lottery,
the prize to be delivered by flaming chariots,
will delight me?
Somehow I have arranged to deny myself
a thousand daily moments of delight. Why?
The mystery deepens.
Love is personal, impersonal
and probably a lot more than that, too.
What about all the people
who have labored on my behalf
even though they did not know me personally?
Filled with self-giving love
some doctor gave himself malaria
so that I and others might be spared.
When you start to think about it
the world is full of countless good-hearted people
past and present, who have labored

to nurture our lives
without knowing us personally,
inventing, along the way,
human language, agriculture, medicine, music.
What sort of life would I have without them?
(I would not be here.)

What would I lose by opening myself
to feel grateful to them? What would I lose
by experiencing these gifts *as love?!*
It is a fact as solid as a brick
that without the Sun, the Earth,
myriad ancestors, my mixed up parents,
countless teachers, do-gooders and helpers,
including those who grow my food
and the truckers who haul it all over creation,
I would not have a life!

Green Cathedral   Fractal painting by Vicky Brago-Mitchell

(Ordinary facts are just plain true
but the fact that you and I are the recipients,
even in lives that include much pain,
of all this amazing grace
is a truth that becomes truer
as we open ourselves to embrace it.)

It's another one of those paradoxes:
imagination actually serves the cause of realism.
To the often-repeated truth that
the map is not the territory
we must a complementary truth:
the blueprint becomes the building.
There are many times and situations where
you can only *receive* as much as you can *conceive*.

In the prayers I am trying to imagine
what has already happened
but is beyond my grasp.

In the prayers I am visualizing
the most intense blessings I can imagine
partly to make room for all the amazing blessings
I have already received
partly to make room for new ones.
(Who knows how many blessings
are struggling this very moment
to make their way into my life
through the tiny opening I have made for them?!)

Every beautiful flower I have ever seen,
every wonderful sunset I have ever marveled at,
every act of kindness I have been lucky enough
to receive or perform,
every warm embrace I have ever experienced,
is alive inside of me somewhere.

How is it that I allow all these experiences
to be driven into the shadow of unknowing
by the daily parade of bad news?
Perhaps I could become
more of a <u>source</u> of good news in my world
rather than seeing myself only
as a recipient of bad news.

And perhaps after warming up in this way
I will be more able to accept
even the difficult challenges of my life
as blessings also... *the far edge of gratitude*

The hope in these new prayers
is to return to, to recreate
the feelings of being loved and cared for
so vividly and so intensely that we feel inspired
to nurture others with that same love and kindness,
to pass on the candle flame.
We have a deep part to play in how this happens.

Rainbow Bodhisattva
painting by Vijali on the wall of a cave in Tibet

CHAPTER TWO

STEPS TOWARD A THEOLOGY OF CONTINUING INCARNATION

In this essay I invite you to join me as I explore two kinds of new thinking in relation to the spiritual dimension of life. First I want to push beyond the boundaries of thing-related thinking (tree, moon, spoon) and think about God as flow, movement and pattern. Although this may sound impersonal, these flows and movements can be quite intimate: life-giving, energizing, connecting, forgiving, awareness-expanding, insight-awakening, and more. One ongoing problem in theology is that the word for "person" is a noun in European languages, so that God as a person gets placed in the same part of our brains as pots, pans and planets: separate objects in space and time.

Second, I want to explore some possibilities of living prayerfully, as distinct from praying. Now I am a person who both prays and encourages others to pray. But my experience is that the Divine Presence always leads us deeper, and that every prayer is a point on a pilgrimage of endless unfolding. So in the second part of this essay I share some of my experience of praying as if God were a verb.

BEYOND DIVINE STUFF

In every age and every culture, people use ideas from everyday life in order to make sense about God and the spiritual life. European-based cultures have for centuries used the idea of substance, *real stuff*, as a way of understanding the reality of God. Ideas of substance, substantial, and enduring being have been the glue that has held most Western theologies together. And along with them, commonsense notions about *quantity*: how a big pile of stuff, gold coins for example, is more significant than a small pile.

Since people do have the experience of the apparent solidity of people and things in everyday life, they will probably continue to think of God as *really there*, the way your best friend is *really there* across the room. In the past century, however, scientists have discovered that everything in the universe is based on real movement and real energy flow rather than real stuff. Atoms are mostly empty space but full of energy and movement. At this very moment, millions of neutrinos, energy bundles from outer space, are passing all the way through your body as if it were not there.

Centuries before any challenges came from science, theologians themselves worked out many of the limitations involved in thinking of God as a separate, substantial being who is "over there." *Ground of Being* replaced *separate being* as the deepest thought people could think about God. This idea allowed people to think of God as still substantial but not separate; *really there* because God is *every where.*

For many thoughtful people today, twentieth century physics has made more and more unworkable those spiritual analogies and understandings based on the idea of substance. If there are no true substances in the universe, only *repeatable experiences* of specific energy flows, then it makes less and less sense to praise God as the most sublime and substantial separate being there ever was. But the same twentieth century physics that dissolved our idea of substantiality has provided us with a rich set of ideas about energy flow, resonance, order underlying chaos, and fractal patterns of organization (like the branching of a tree limb) that repeat again and again at different levels of scale.

The Shape of Forever
Fractal painting by Vicky Brago-Mitchell

Far from making spiritual thoughts unthinkable, I have found that these ideas from science can allow us to look at ancient truths with new eyes, and understand them in new and amazing ways.

In a substance-oriented way of thinking, for example, what sense can be made out of the teaching that human beings are made "in the image and likeness of God?" Thing-thinking must lead us inevitably toward images of a God who has arms and legs! Or to search inside of ourselves for some invisible God-stuff.

But "fractal-flow"-oriented thinking would lead us in a very different direction, Fractals are patterns in nature and mathematics that repeat at many levels of size. The arteries that leave your heart branch and branch again, down to the smallest capillary. Thus do rivers merge from the smallest streams and tree limbs branch to the smallest twig. "Branching" is a repeating pattern of activity. And the turning of the spiral turns the same, from its center to its widest rim.

When you start to observe how there are repeating patterns of activity all through nature, patterns wherein small and large move in similar ways, it is no longer so outlandish to think that when we move through a day mercifully, kindly and awarely, that the qualities of our actions may be deeply related to some Larger Pattern of Movement which is flowing Mercifully, Kindly and Awarely through us. The fractal forms that are everywhere around us suggest a universal theology of incarnating adverbs.

Adverbs, through which we express such qualities of action as "generously" and "forgivingly," are the most ethereal forms of speech, lighter than an angel's wing. It is a beautiful paradox to me that these least substantial words in our lives might open doorways to life's deepest meanings.

I urge you to study how the large and the small are related all around you through the process of "branching": in ferns, in broccoli florets, in the veins of a maple leaf and your own hands, in the roots of every plant on the planet. Then go back and meditate on the teaching that human beings are made "in the image and likeness of God." Instead of encountering a static image, you may find yourself feeling deeply connected to something much larger than yourself, a flow of energy and activity that invites you deeper into the heart of life.

In a tree, the smallest twig branches in exactly the same way as the largest limb. By analogy, you may think of yourself as "not much" spiritually, merely a twig. But the fractal similarity of the large and the small suggests that you may have inner resources of which you are unaware, which can not be measured in terms of quantity, but only of quality. When Mother Teresa said that we are not given to do great things in this life, but to do small things with great love, she was giving a fractal teaching in which the quality matters but the size does not.

These ideas about fractal patterns of activity would be at the heart of a new theology of Incarnating Adverbs. If life and people and the entire universe are patterned flows of activity rather than substantial things, then the qualities we want in our lives are best represented by adverbs, words like lovingly, forgivingly, awarely, delightedly. When we speak of these qualities in the noun forms of love, forgiveness, awareness, etc., we use a language of separate objects (house, tree, brick) that unconsciously holds these qualities at some distance from ourselves. When we speak and think and pray using the adverbial forms we invite these qualities to enter into us more fully, because these adverbial qualities can attach themselves to, and merge with, almost all of our actions, thoughts, feelings and intentions.

Stated somewhat more systematically, this Theology of Incarnating Adverbs seems to me to propose the following web of ideas:

It is helpful to think of God as flowing energy and activity, imbued with an infinite number of infinitely beautiful qualities, rather than as a static object. More like an amazingly beautiful chord of music, rather than a ball of sublime stuff.

It is helpful to think of ourselves as flowing energy and activity, endlessly changing and therefore always capable of growing more fully into the expression of the Divine qualities, rather than as static objects. This is true even if the language of movement and flow sounds cumbersome to the ear when we first use it.

The very small is capable of expressing the very large, in a way that is similar to process by which the smallest strings on a harp hum with the tones played on the largest strings. There is a real transfer of energy and information between the large strings and the small ones, and in a similar way, people often experience themselves as energized when they encounter others who are animated by great compassion and/or profound understanding.

God continues to incarnate in us as we shape the qualities of our moment to moment activity to be in resonance with the Divine qualities as best we understand them. (Or, alternately, one might see this relationship as that we continue to give birth to God as we express ever more fully the beautiful qualities hidden in the as yet unmanifest God-flow.)

Our knowledge and embodiment of the Divine qualities will probably never be final and do not need to be final, because part of the perfection of the Divine is an inexhaustible power to give birth to something new, and an inexhaustible yearning to be made ever more manifest. Endlessly new chords of beauty and meaning can emerge as the qualities of the Divine Flowing are woven together again and again in our lives. Our assignment from the universe is to love with a new and greater love, to see with a new and greater vision, to create with a new and deeper creativity, and so on.

Like seeds cast upon the wind, our assignment is to plant ourselves somewhere and cast new seeds of compassion and delight upon future winds. Knowing this we can hold all our ideas about the spiritual life as working approximations, necessarily open to endless refinement as the process toward which our ideas point, evolves. The reward for adopting this attitude of approximation and reverential non-finality is the freedom to grow.

And, finally, **the fundamental unit of human experiencing** does not have to be the day or even the minute, but instead **could be understood as a single breathing in and breathing out.** There are approximately twelve to eighteen thousand breathings in a person's waking day. Each breathing can express all of the qualities of the God-flow. We can breathe gratefully, forgivingly, awarely, compassionately, delightedly, energizingly, nurturingly, creatively, and so on as the infinitely giving presence sings through our living.

FRACTAL MANTRAS OF INCARNATION

I hope these thoughts will invite you to see each present moment with new eyes, and to feel your own moment-to-moment actions as openings through which the Divine Breathing can be ever more fully born into this world... deeply peacefully, endlessly compassionately, creatively expressively, gratefully delightedly, and more!

Here is a meditation that I have been doing for several years on these themes: Sit or lay quietly, focus on your breathing and gently repeat in your mind any two of the adverbs in the paragraphs above or on the list below. Feel your way into the qualities. Play some slow, rhythmic music if it helps. You can also think of the saints or exemplars whose lives have embodied these qualities.

The rainbow can be understood as an archetypal
symbol of incarnation: the beauty of heaven comes to Earth

What would it feel like to breathe more courageously, more generously? Could you do it for just one breath? Because if you can do it for just one breath, then you can do it ever more deeply for a lifetime. You can breathe more creatively and compassionately in, through and under all you're your various activities in living. Fractal imagery suggests that what is most beautiful in you could be expressed in your smallest, plainest moments. Each of what you may see as your "ordinary" moments is really like a flower, waiting to open up. What it needs is some sunlight from your heart.

Well, that is the expanding world of exploration into which I invite you. And the qualities of what one might call the Heart of God turn out to be in many respects the qualities of a fully developing person, the many-sided fractal, I believe, of a continuing incarnation participated in by Jesus, Buddha, the saints of all religions and every compassionate and aware person who has ever lived (as well as all animal species in which compassion, awareness and creativity are emerging!).

I thought about this for many years and finally decided to try to write down as many of the qualities as I could. The following list is drawn from my own experience and my encounters with many wisdom traditions, ancient and modern, (among which there is actually a lot of agreement). You will recognize the influence of Jesus, St. Paul and St. Francis on this list, along with Carl Rogers, Abraham Maslow, Martin Buber, Erik Erikson, and Gautama Buddha. In compiling this synthesis, I have translated all the fixed qualities of character described by these various teachers into ways of action, consistent with the idea that the universe is a flow rather than a thing, and we also are a moving stream.

Thus translated into adverbs (and grouped into related clusters), we can say that at every stage along life's way we are challenged to think, act, dream, and interact with one another in the following ways...

... more awarely (of self, other and context)

... more skillfully, competently and wisely

... more honestly, sincerely, genuinely, congruently (inner matches outer)

... more caringly, compassionately, acceptingly, respectfully, warmly, forgivingly

... more creatively and "exploratorily" (with more creative openness to new experience)

... more courageously, hopefully and faithfully

... more generously and nurturingly, delighting in the happiness of others

... more meaningfully and expressively, organizing and expressing our experiences in coherent patterns of words, music, movement and imagery

... more gratefully and appreciatively, open to delight

... more engagingly, energetically and responsively

... more gracefully and beautifully (in the Navajo sense of beauty as cosmic harmony)

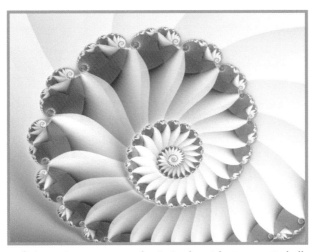

Infinite Stairway   Fractal painting by Vicky Brago-Mitchell

As you walk through each day, you can let your breathing remind you of the beautiful qualities wanting to be expressed <u>this moment</u>. Just as practice and improvisation go hand in hand in piano playing, a structured, almost rosary-like focus on the Incarnating Adverbs can go hand in hand with a spontaneous opening of oneself to bring into each new situation just that chord of qualities needed. I find that the two-adverb combinations continue to inspire and startle me with new possibilities: creatively forgivingly, courageously responsively, and so on. There are hundreds of combinations and taken together they represent a kind of evolving map of God-as-flowing, God-as-love-incarnating. For me, the idea of Incarnation is profoundly dynamic and cannot be contained or limited. When Jesus taught his followers to pray "Thy will be done on earth as it is in heaven," it seems to me that he was, and is, inviting us all into a life of continuous incarnational development. "On earth" includes me, here, now. And many beautiful saints, sages and mystics of many religions have expressed this same extraordinary invitation, an invitation made suddenly new by our evolving understanding that the very small can express the very large.

The prayerful meditation on the Incarnating Adverbs that I have shared with you in this essay is my way of opening up <u>this moment</u>, again and again, as the doorway into which eternity can enter. To me it is the lost half of the process of prayer. For just as much as we need to have distinct moments of prayer and meditation that are in contrast to our everyday activity, we also need ways to bring the energy and awareness of prayer into each moment of our everyday activity,

creatively... and delightfully.

Skylight Window in the Great Mosque of Isfahan

CHAPTER THREE

THOUGHTS ON THE LIFE OF BLESSING

may your heart be a window
through which endless blessings
pour into the world

In the spring of 1975 the life of blessing opened to me. I would like to tell you the story of how it happened.

So many events in my life have been paradoxical, and this was, too. Obstacles turn into treasures. Treasures turn into obstacles.

I was a religious studies student at the time, and taking a class on religion and science at the University of California at Santa Barbara. We were assigned to read one of the most obscure but hopeful books of the twentieth century: *The Phenomenon of Man*, by the Jesuit paleontologist, philosopher and mystic, Pierre Teilhard de Chardin. It is also one of the most ambitious books ever written, in that Teilhard hoped to explain the evolution and destiny *of the entire universe,* ourselves included.

And to handle this giant theme, Teilhard invented an entire vocabulary of giant words, words like noogenesis (the birth of mind), orthogenesis, cosmogenesis and Christogenesis, that rang with the feeling of deep meaning even if we didn't quite know what they meant. I plunged into the book and was quickly in way over my head. The weeks raced by. A test loomed. I spent more and more hours in intense concentration, trying to see the pattern of meaning hidden behind these truly cosmic words. My life became like a monastic retreat, a sleepless Zen ordeal in which I wrestled continuously with an unanswerable riddle. The giant words began to divide in my mind and recombine in new variants. Things were getting out of control. I tried harder.

I never did understand Teilhard that well, but something wonderful happened. After weeks of effort, I gave up. And in the quiet that followed giving up, a simple picture took shape in my mind. The picture included a big tuning fork (a u-shaped piece of metal that rings with a specific tone when you strike it), and a little tuning fork. The diagram, which you could have drawn on a matchbook cover, was an answer, not to the question about the destiny of life on Earth, but instead, an answer to my personal questions about the spiritual life. (The little diagram may say something about the destiny of life on Earth, but that is another story.) In a moment, an entire series of linked thoughts flashed across my mind.

The big tuning fork represented God, the small tuning fork represented me. If you strike the big one to make a tone, a middle C, for example, and the little one is tuned to a multiple of the same frequency, the little one will hum along. This is what gives pianos their rich sound. Many strings hum along in a complex chord of resonance. Energy transfers from the large strings to the small ones. I had the feeling that I was on to something.

What would it mean for me to tune my life to God's life? If you thought of the Divine Presence as some sort of extraordinarily beautiful music, what would I need to do to enter into a "resonant" relationship with It. The answer seemed very straightforward: I should try to do in a small way whatever I believed most deeply that God is doing in a big way.

And what did I believe that God was doing in a big way? I thought of a mother holding a newborn child and the answer came: God is pouring out a stream of blessings, like a mother, or like the sunlight. God is pouring out His/Her being into our being the way the Sun pours out its substance as light upon the grasses and the trees. If God is loving and blessing all of us into existence, then "getting in tune" with God would mean to love and bless everyone around me. (These are all ancient themes. They somehow all came alive in me in a single moment. Tibetans sometimes speak of how a single flash of lightning can allow you to see where everything is in a darkened room.)

Vision of Divine Energy
Fractal painting by Bourbaki

I was deeply drawn to theme of blessing. The sunlight calls forth the plant hidden in the seed, parents' love calls forth the person-to-be hidden in the baby. In blessing there is often a calling forth of something hidden, something not yet accomplished. You are ill and I hold you in my mind as capable of becoming completely well again. You are out of a job, and I bless you to find a job that is right for you, which is to say, I give voice to what is not yet, I hold my mind open to new possibilities in your life during the times when it is difficult for you to imagine them. I give thanks for you, even when you are having difficult time giving thanks for your own life. It does not have to be all pastel. I bless many people I meet to find new meaning in the terrible events that have shaped their lives. We seem to serve others best when we both share their sorrows and bear gentle witness to the hope and joy that the sorrow has temporarily eclipsed. I say <u>gentle</u> witness because the purpose of blessing is not to hurry others through their troubles. I see the purpose of blessing as this: to be a deeply accepting bridge between what is now and what could be, to stand in the now and make a gentle, inviting space for the new. These are some of the understandings that have, in the last two decades, grown around the original impulse to bless and the analogy of the tuning forks.

Beyond the crises and sorrows of everyday life, this calling forth of the plant hidden within the seed repeats at many levels. In the months and years after my awakening to blessing, I began to practice prayers of blessing every day.

For it is as though we are on an infinite stairway, and however far we may have traveled, there is still more love, beauty, awareness, creativity, and so on, waiting to be brought forth. The point is not, if I may be allowed to disagree with the Apostle Paul, that we have all fallen short of the glory of God. From a religious evolutionary perspective, the point is that the glory of God is open-ended. It is our reaching and growing toward it, rather than our failure to reach it, that is important. These prayers of blessing took on a life of their own in my mind and heart. In the early 1980s, perhaps in response to some science fiction novels I had been reading, my spontaneous prayers became galactic. "May love and wisdom blossom forth on a trillion, trillion worlds" came again and again into my heart. What do I imagine God is up to, holding all the galaxies in Her Infinite Lap? How is it that something as improbable as maternal love has emerged on so many branches of the tree of life? The Prayer of St. Francis begins by saying, "Lord, make me an instrument of your peace." In what various ways could I cooperate with that process?

In more recent years my blessings have become more down-to-earth. "May every heart be filled with infinite kindness." And they have become more personal: "May every heart be filled with infinite kindness, including mine."

I have come to feel that blessings should be expressed in language that is culturally familiar. To some of my friends I say, "I am visualizing you surrounded by healing angels." Others are not particularly fond of angel imagery. To them I say "I am visualizing you surrounded by healing sparkles." One issue here is that our vocabulary for describing <u>what is</u> does not adequately express <u>what is coming</u>, <u>what is being born</u>, or the <u>directions in which something might unfold</u>. We need both vocabularies, but it seems to me that in today's world we are suffering from the inability to articulate new possibilities. Blessing is like watering seeds that are hidden under the ground. A person who had never seen a garden might say, "What a silly fellow. Why is he pouring water on the barren ground?"

And as you go deeper into the life of blessing, you begin to feel how it is that the love that comes through you also comes to you. On the surface, the waves look separate; in the depths, there is just one ocean. (I have learned, in the years since 1975, that earnestly wishing the infinite well being of all sentient beings is at the heart of Tibetan spiritual life.)

Another example comes to mind. Your body and mind may be capable of many extraordinary things, but if you think of them as robots, you will never find out what those extraordinary things might be. Blessing is a way of making friends with the universe, near and far. I bless each of your sixty trillion cells to be full of light, I bless each one to cooperate with all the others, for the highest good of you and everyone. Can you imagine that??? If you can't imagine that, I appeal to you take the leap, to take the next step. In the short run, thoughts like this may seem to make no difference at all. In the long run, they may make all the difference. The practice of blessing is a gentle and happy yoga of the heartmind.

In blessing we try to cooperate with the flows of energy that have come together to give us life. Although some of my blessings may sound outlandish, there is an element of deep humility in them. It is a humility that says, "The creative processes of Life / God / the Buddhamind / the Universe, are not finished with you and they are not finished with me. I open myself to cooperate with them anew, no matter how foolish I may look or sound along the way."

We see how, in the many branches of the tree of life, loving attention nurtures human babies and wolf cubs and (for a few crucial moments) even crocodile hatchlings. Something is going on out there, amid the chaos of conflict and competition. In blessing, we reach to say it out loud. We reach to say the word of endless kindness that is <u>saying us</u> into existence, that we might say others into existence. And in works of blessing, in every act of mercy and reconciliation, we incarnate (and surrender to) a love evolving in the marrow of life.

I invite you to explore the life of blessing, and to find the blessing within you that is deeply yours to bestow upon the people and animals and plants around you. I bless and invite you to see yourself as a large, open window through which more blessings can pour into the world. In my theology of the two tuning forks, the universe wants to sing its song of infinite blessing through every heart, through every mind, and through every pair of hands, at work in works of lovingkindness, <u>yours and mine included</u>.

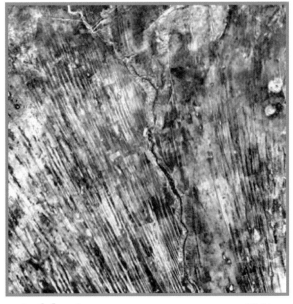

Earth from Space   NASA

Pilgrim   Marion C. Honors

CHAPTER FOUR

AN ECOLOGY OF DEVOTION
(first published in EarthLight Magazine, Summer 2003)

Somewhere in his essays about the ecological crises of our time, I remember Wendell Berry writing "What we do not love, we will not save." One of the many possible implications that I draw from his statement is that the eco-spiritual life is breath-like: the more we want to reach out to nurture the web of life (and save our own species along the way), the more deeply we will need to journey into our own hearts to connect with love's sustaining energy.

Although Planet Earth needs love the way a person lost in the desert needs water, love cannot be summoned by a simple act of will. Love, in my experience, is not like an object already in our possession, that we could give if we chose to do so. Love seems to me much more like a garden that will eventually bear fruit if cultivated in a spirit of apprenticeship, taking the time to learn about each tree and plant.

In this essay I will explore a five-fold vision of what might be called an ecology of devotion: a way of seeing how our various loves, concerns, gratitudes, adorations and celebrations are all part of a larger organic unity.

These many loves and concerns call to us, often in a chaotic din, urging us forward in many directions, appealing to us at many levels: friends need comfort, a new baby is born, the forests are dying, the dolphins are beaching, millions of landmines wait silently for human or animal footstep. Where and how shall we turn toward life and begin (or continue) the labors of "mending the world," the *Tikkun Olam* of Jewish tradition, which would also constitute the mending of our own broken hearts? As I have experienced the web of life being threatened by the explosive mix of greed, fear and technology, I have been challenged to find inside myself a love stronger than all fears, a deeper reverence for life that could be my compass through the chaos of a world unraveling.

Over the past year, in dialogue with a community of supportive friends called Turn Toward Life, I have been exploring a kind of mental rosary of our various loves and devotions, reverences that span the spectrum from gratitude to care to adoration. Like a garland with five flowers arranged in a circle, this five-fold rosary holds the various loves that struggle to be born in me. Here is how I see them, and how I will discuss them in the pages that follow:

reverence for the life that lives within us,

reverence for the life that unfolds between us,

reverence for the life that surrounds and sustains us,

reverence for all the life of the future,

reverence for the source of all life.

Stained-glass window at Chartres cathedral. The interior of
a cathedral can be understood, from a Jungian point of view,
as symbolic of the deepest reaches of the inner life of the self.

1. Reverence for the life that lives within us.

The closest life for which we can have reverence is the life that lives within us, our breathing, moving seeing, hearing, tasting, hoping, loving, yearning, and reaching; all the direct experiences of being alive, and those moments, often out in nature, when we suddenly feel good about being alive. I remember as a child the thrill, the exuberance, the infinite, bodily well-being, of running down a long beach near my house.

The Universe has labored mightily that we might breathe, and see the light of morning. The calcium, carbon and iron that support these processes were made in the hearts of ancient stars. The caloric energy that lets us run is compressed starlight, the light of the sun conveyed to us from leaf to corn and wheat through countless hands.

I have never felt more alive in my life than when I have been in love. For most of my life I took these feelings as revelations about the person with whom I was in love. Only in recent years have I begun to realize that these feeling were also saying something to me about my capacity to love, inviting me to get more acquainted with my own heart, with this intense aliveness. How is it that compressed starlight found this way of expressing itself? At times in my life I have complained bitterly to the Universe that love was not more evident in life. At some point the gestalt shifted and I suddenly realized how extraordinary it was that a universe composed mostly of rock and gas could have given birth to any experience of love, anywhere. And even more extraordinary was the fact that I was a carrier of this capacity, however clumsily I might carry it.

Our seemingly mundane existence, looked at from this angle, is a miracle of mind-boggling proportions. However ordinary or unworthy we may feel, we are nonetheless recipients of this galactic grace. Coming to understand how much we have received, beyond any measure of earning (for who could earn sunlight, or a billion years of evolution), sets the stage for us to give something back to life out of the fullness of gratitude, delight and awe. We are the Milky Way with arms and legs, eyes and ears, and hearts yearning to love. What will we create with the creative energy that the Universe has poured into us?

2. Reverence for the life that lives between us

There is a paradox at the heart of human unfolding: We can only love others to the degree that we are capable of loving ourselves. But, on the other hand, we are not born loving ourselves; we develop self-love by internalizing the love of all those who have loved us. As infants, we do not make our own food; neither do we make our own love.

Later in life, having been given the template, we may become bestowers of kindness; having been fed, we will feel the rightness of feeding others; having been nurtured by many along the way, we will find a way to nurture others.

Like day and night, summer and winter, the nature that lives and breathes through us is full of polarities. I come into the fullness of MY personal being in relation to many YOUs. To cherish life at a deeper level is to accept this web of interwovenness, of land and sea, yes... of lake and forest, yes...but also, of you and me. This fragile human co-arising is as much a part of nature as spiderweb, wildebeeste or waterfall.

The life that emerges between us... The partnership of bodies brings forth new bodies. The partnership of minds, brings forth new minds. Hearts joined in love invite everyone to love more. "Love one another," Jesus said, "as I have loved you," not only counseling his followers but also describing the path love travels down the generations, if we let it, because we let it. So also do hatred and oppression travel down the generations.

The Kiss   Constantin Brancusi

And how beyond the circle of our human lives, one well might ask, is this related to ecology and reverence for life? In more ways than one would imagine. Perhaps the most dramatic link is that our human conflicts are having catastrophic impacts on other species. Driven by greed and unskilled in sharing, human beings are emptying the sea of fish and emptying the mountains of trees. Elephants in the jungles and forests of Indochina step on landmines just as people do. Our fears of our enemies, and their fears of us, have left the world awash in nuclear waste, which damages the gene-pools of human and animal alike. Ultimately, as Wendell Berry observes, we treat the natural world with the same love or disregard that we bestow on one another:

> *The Earth is all we have in common. We cannot damage it without damaging those with whom we share it. There is an uncanny resemblance between*

our behavior with each other and our behavior toward the earth. The willingness to exploit one becomes the willingness to exploit the other. It is impossible to care for each other more or differently than we care for the earth.

To cherish the web of life, to protect life, it is now clear that we must necessarily face the shadow side of our own temperaments and our own cultures, the life that unfolds between us. For it is we humans, moved by various greeds and fears in relation to one another, who make and use these technologies of contamination and death.

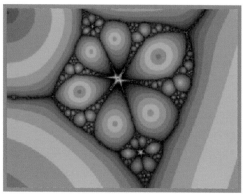

Fractal of Life   Mark King

The extremity of our predicament -- that we are destroying our own life-support system as we drive many species over the brink of extinction -- draws us toward the life that lives between us, not only as a source of despair, but also as a source of hope. Just as it is true that two together can carry a larger object than either would be able to carry alone, it is also true that in the company of supportive friends we can bear sorrows that are more than one heart can contain. I have become deeply convinced that creating an ecologically sustainable civilization will require creating a web of emotionally sustaining friendships, full of gratitude, listening and celebration. Gandhi would say start with yourself, be the change you want to see. A more intimate way of expressing this might be to say, embody the love, gratitude and compassion you want to promote.

3. Reverence for the life that surrounds and sustains us

This is the dimension of reverence for life that is most familiar to us, having been lived and expressed so beautifully by such eco-advocates as Albert Schweitzer, Rachel Carson, Jane Goodall, John Muir, Matthew Fox, Joanna Macy and Thomas Berry. Along with being great lovers of nature, these guiding lights were and are great students of nature.

A path of devotion in relation to the web of life around us is something more than just having a well of good feelings toward all creatures great and small, although that would be a great place to start. Feelings arise out of understandings. The more we understand about the history of each bite of food we take, the more likely we are to be filled with awe and gratitude. The more we know of fruit trees, the more each peach feels like a miracle. But if all of this is true, and the path toward a respectful partnership with the rest of nature is so straightforward, why is the world still falling apart. What is the problem? What follows is one approach to an answer.

Early in the twentieth century, the philosopher Martin Buber introduced what may be one of the most important distinctions in the history of human thought. Buber proposed that human beings do not have a sense of "I" in isolation. Rather, we have a sense of "I" in relation to either _someone_ or _something_. When we relate to another person as having experiences, feelings and purposes in the same way we do, we have an "I-Thou" sense of self. We strive to acknowledge the other person as an end in themselves, not merely as a means to the satisfaction of our own needs or desires.

When we relate to an object that we experience as having no will, desire or consciousness of its own, we have an "I-It" sense of ourselves in relation to that object. We see the object as material for our use, as is often the case in relation to wood, food, oil, the ground that bears food, and members of ethnic groups other than our own. Buber acknowledged that we could not survive without using at least some of the objects in our world to sustain our lives. But he felt that we become truly human only when we are able to grant humanness to others, are able to feel others as worthy of our care and not just see others as sources of care, food, resources, power, status, etc. A healthy person would shift back and forth as appropriate, not treating a chair as if it were a person, but also not treating a person as if he or she were a chair.

Life Intertwined   Lila-Hog

The decades that followed the publication of Buber's book, *I and Thou*, developed the "I-Thou" and "I-It" ideas in two important ways. Within the field of human development, significant thinkers concluded that the ability to value other people as ends in themselves, distinct from oneself and yet worthy of care, was one of the central features of mature human development. (In this, they came to agree with medieval theologians.) And in the field of psychotherapy, there was a related realization that the inability to feel the personhood of others, as a consequence of severely disturbed early relationships, was one of the major character disorders of our era (including the "narcissistic personality"). People suffering from narcissistic personality disorder experience an inflated sense of entitlement in which everyone and everything are reduced to the status of furniture to be used at will. (Think of a mountain with all the trees cut down.)

I have given this extended introduction to Buber's ideas about the "I-Thou" and "I-It" ways of being a person because they describe the central area of problems for people in societies experiencing runaway industrialization.

Runaway industrialization turns every person, plant and animal on Planet Earth into a heap of inert raw material, into psychologically dead stuff, all the better to plan for how it may all be used for the only source of purpose and value left in the world: more profits in capitalist societies, more power -- the triumph of the state -- in totalitarian ones. This is the "I-It" sense of self writ large across the world, leaving behind a trail of clear-cut mountains and flooded lowlands. Capitalism, communism and totalitarianism agree deeply on one thing: living nature is really just dead stuff in motion, therefore we may do with it whatever we please.

The problem with this view is that, from a Buberian perspective, in "deadening" or de-personalizing the world in order to use it for our ends, we have deadened and depersonalized ourselves. We harden ourselves to not feel the pain of whomever and whatever we use, exploit and/or consume. And once having thus hardened, deadened and depersonalized ourselves, no amount of cars and refrigerators and 60-inch television sets can ever make us happy. We may not even feel the ecological cliff toward which we are racing.

In his book, *The Dream of the Earth*, Thomas Berry describes how interwoven our personal development is with the web of life on Planet Earth. To grow up in a world that includes whales and tigers and elephants is to have evoked in oneself a very specific sense of beauty and majesty. When those creatures are gone, that specific sense will be gone, and the personhood of humanity will be radically diminished.

Seeing the no-win nature of the "I-It" path can be a shock, but can also free us to explore more sustainable and fulfilling ways of living. There are two sides to this realization: a warning and a promise. The warning is that whatever we inflict upon the world around us we inflict upon ourselves in a variety of ways. The promise, full of transformational possibilities, is also two-fold:

First, the more value, beauty, depth of experience and purpose that we recognize and nurture in the world around us, the more of these we will be able to recognize and nurture in ourselves and in one another.

And the converse is also true: the more value, beauty, depth of experience and purpose that we recognize and nurture in one another, the more of these we will be able to recognize and nurture in the larger web of life around us.

This suggests to me an almost-haiku:

> *start where you are,*
> *the path*
> *is wherever you are standing*

4. Reverence for all the life of the future

Like a pregnant woman big with child, the web of life today holds all future generations of life on Earth. Life blossoms forth through an endless spiral of eternal pregnancy, birthgiving, nurturing, coming together (of earth and seed, of egg and sperm) to begin again, and dying away to make way for the new.

Into this steady progression of ebbs and flows something new has entered, something that holds both promise and peril. In recent eras of evolution, *evolution itself has begun to evolve,* evolving from adaptation to adaptability, from the perfectly adapted claw to the hand and brain that can learn many new ways of holding many new things, and the evolution of a temperament to love one's offspring and teach them these new ways of holding.

Pregnant Woman   Sigrid Herr

We humans are not alone in this development; we share this evolution toward learning and creativity with many species, especially our primate brothers and sisters, chimpanzees, gorillas and bonobos. And we are far from fully understanding of the intelligence of creatures quite different from us, such as dolphins and bee colonies. But we have gone further on this path of open adaptability, as far as we know, than any other species, and therefore our freedom and capacity to make catastrophic mistakes is much greater than that of any other species. No other creature, for example, leaves behind leaking piles of radioactive waste, slowly destroying the genetic integrity of all life as the radioactive contaminants circulate more and more widely through the biosphere.

Because we alone have developed the power to destroy all life, we alone are challenged to love all creatures intensely enough to want to save them, to love all creatures intensely enough to be willing to restrain our own appetites, to understand our own hatred and greeds. That, I submit to you, is a very intense devotion, a transformational gratitude, and, paradoxically, in this era of technological might, that all-embracing love has become the assignment of every human heart. As the cosmologist Brian Swimme has noted, from the point of view of species extinction our present era is the worst time in the last sixty-five million years. Without some deep trans-formation, it is not clear how life on Earth will continue. If there are going to be living plants and birds and fish and human beings in the future, it will be because we work to protect the seeds of their existence today, and the land and water that will make their lives possible. It will be because we open our hearts to love them now.

5. Reverence for the source of all life

In this exploration of reverence for life, I have deliberately shifted among a family of related words: love, reverence, devotion, gratitude, respect, service, celebration, nurture, protection, adoration. Other times and cultures would add such words as *agape, bhakti, karuna* and *caritas.* I used this wide variety of words out of my feeling that reverence for life is larger and more complex than any one word would suggest.

I am deeply convinced, for example, that when we reach toward the source of all life, we are also reaching toward the ultimate source of love, because love is the core of our aliveness.

In a fertile arc of self-referentiality, our capacity to love life is something that life itself is exploring and developing!

Spiral Galaxy   Image Courtesy NASA

As children it is very difficult for us to imagine how we might have come out of our parents' bodies. Later we understand that, but struggle to bring into focus the way our personalities emerged from the matrix of personalities surrounding us when we were young. Eventually, we face the deepest mystery of all: how all of us, the family of life together, are continuously emerging out of the womb of an endlessly pregnant Universe. In the galactic unfolding of life, the life webs and planets that may survive are those who learn to love and nurture the ongoing miracle of their own co-emergence!

As our reverence for life deepens, it often deepens to include that something (or someone) larger than us, of which our lives are felt to be a creative and loving expression. The influence of science over the last few centuries has been to rule out such feelings of connectedness to something larger, because the science of that era could only look <u>down</u> the scale of connectedness at what were understood as our "parts" and how those alleged parts were hitched together. In truth, none of our alleged parts, heart, brain, liver, and so on, are as separate as they appear at first glance. They are all interwoven.

The emerging science looks both up and down and asks: what larger system enfolds this element (you and me), and how does this element function in relation to that larger system? Parts imply wholes, as your hand implies every bit of the rest of you, raising the extraordinary questions of what *we together* imply and what life implies.

We may never be able to fully grasp the larger system that enfolds us, but we have many hints and many suggestive analogies. Consider the fern in your garden. The tiniest part of a fern leaf bears the shape of the entire fern branch. When we turn to nature, we find that there are many such "fractal" examples, from trees to rivers to blood vessels, in which the very small mirrors the shape and function of the very large. So it is much more thinkable today than it was half a century ago, for us to feel that the noblest impulses in us express a larger nobility that enfolds us.

In my own life my sense of "the larger something of which I am a part" have been deeply influenced by the teaching, affirmed by many faiths using different vocabularies, that "God is love, and whoever dwells in love, dwells in God and God in them" -- a truly fractal mysticism. For me, this teaching of lovingkindness, and the people who have embodied this lovingkindness, complete the spiral ecology of devotion.

In reaching toward the infinite,
I am brought back to my own heart,
to the life that lives within me as love,
to the life reaches toward people and plants
*   and animals as caring,*
to the life in us capable of cherishing
*   the presence in the now*
*   of all future generations.*

Spiral Shell (photographer unknown)

CHAPTER FIVE

DARSHAN IS TO BLESS
WITH EYES AND HEART

Darshan is a spiritual practice from India. Traditionally, it is a form of blessing and open-eyed meditation in which disciples gaze upon the face of their beloved spiritual teacher, and receive her or his gaze in return. It has overtones of loving and being loved, knowing and being known, of standing naked in the light of eternity, since it is commonly held belief in Hindu spiritual communities that one's teacher knows all one's

Charan Singh Mararaj, circa 1955

thoughts, an idea and experience made more vivid by a face to face encounter with that person. There are parallel practices in Sufism and the Sikh faith.

While exploring some new possibilities about eco-spirituality with a friend , I had a moment of awakening. As he looked into my eyes, I suddenly realized that it might be possible for all of us to give Darshan (blessing with the eyes) to one another! (This fits right in with one of my favorite sayings of Paramahansa Yogananda, "After me, Love will be the Guru.")

Contagious blessing. Rather than waiting for the perfect guru to arrive, we might each become a window through which more love could pour into the world. We can look into each other's eyes, and each give the deepest blessing we can express at that moment, a kind of visual unfolding of the meaning of Namaste (the Divine Presence in me bows to the Divine Presence in you). While the practice of such an egalitarian Darshan might violate the hierarchical structure of some spiritual communities, it does not violate the central idea of Hinduism: that your soul is a wave in the ocean of God's being, that you are

Amma, contemporary Hindu saint and guru, in Darshan pose

already one with God but have fallen asleep to that deepest aspect of your true being. (The basic logic of the argument for an evolving, shared, egalitarian Darshan would be that, because the Divine Presence is already IN everyone, then the Divine Presence can certainly bless everyone THROUGH everyone.)

Awakening. There is a growing experience inside of me that the process of darshan has now overflowed the container of the guru-disciple relationship and is making its way through the world from person to person, a kind of beautiful contagion. This started about a year ago when I looked into the eyes of my friend, Richard Page, while sharing a meal at a restaurant near Berkeley, California. (Richard is quite a mystic, and was a follower of Swami Muktananda.) At the same time I am aware from my reading in human development that the process of seeing mama and being seen by mama, is the stairway the baby climbs to become a person.

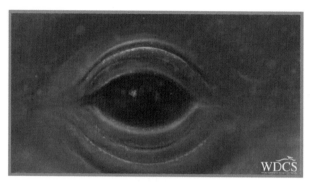

Eye of Blue Whale
(from the Whale and Dolphin Conservation Society -- www.wdcs.org)

And all through life, the process of having some aspect of ourselves seen by another, is a crucial factor in the unfolding of that aspect. I for one see Darshan as a carrying forward of this organic duet. When someone who is aware of themselves *as love and awareness* looks into our eyes, they are likely to awaken our own knowledge of ourselves as love and awareness. As adults we live surrounded by an invisible thought bubble of our own and our culture's making. When someone who does not live in that bubble looks at us, and we look at them, there is a possible moment of awakening and new relatedness.

Living the Light: Our moment in history. Some years ago, in the introduction to my book, *The Geometry of Dialogue*, I pointed out that although the plutonium in a nuclear weapon is 3.5 million times more explosive, pound for pound, than the TNT (or other stuff) it replaces, we have not become 3.5 million times kinder and wiser (a version of something similar that was said by Einstein a long time ago). That contrast, in my view, is the strange and out-of-this-world challenge of being born into this era: to become 3.5 million times kinder, wiser, more creative, more grateful, more forgiving, more able to bring out the best in one another and to help heal the worst. I find it an amazing, terrifying and beautiful moment to be alive. In the history of planet, as far as we know, there has never before been a time in which the power of tools increased by a factor of more than a million within the lifetime of single tool user. How will we rise to this extraordinary occasion? Will we all start to glow in the dark with some sort of spiritual light? When you think about it, the phrase, "glow in the dark," could be taken as a wonderful summary of our life assignment in this world of terror and torture: To bring compassion into a world obsessed with fear and greed, and to remember the love that we were born to live. May each of us live the light ever more fully.

How does energy get awakened inside of people? I am open to the possibility of some sort of "morphic resonance" or "fractal resonance" going on here. When we look into the eyes of another with the intention to bless and/or to receive a blessing, we re-enact and to some unknown degree recreate the baby's first experience of shared loving gaze with mama and papa. At another level, all the shared loving gazes in the history of the universe may be vibrating somewhere like a giant chord perpetually singing on the strings of some transdimensional harp. When we gaze with the intention to bless, the intention to bring out the best in another and ourselves, we may be tuning in to all the moments of Darshan and all the loving gazes that have ever been, spiritual, parental, erotic, romantic, and on and on, the whole universe in a moment.

Aung San Suu Kyi (winner of the 1991 Nobel Peace Prize)
Prime Minister-Elect of Myanmar(Burma)
(under house arrest by military for many years)

I am including in this chapter what seem to me to be Darshan photos and paintings. Some are of spiritual teachers, some are of animals (spiritual teachers in their own right), some are of people in whose gaze I feel some greater presence calling. Of course, one might protest: How can you receive Darshan from a painting?! But if you look at from the point of view of fractal resonance, even a painting or drawing might allow our minds to tune in to a particular frequency, to be informed by a particular form, to sing the same melody. (I am comfortable with all such metaphors, because it is so clear to me that they are *empowering* and *illuminating* metaphors, rather than *mere* metaphors.)

Fractal transmission of compassion. There is some sort of transmission of spiritual energy involved in this that I can only understand at the intuitive level. ("Transmission" is one paradigm, "evoking" is another. Perhaps the transmission is *through* evoking: I don't actually give it to you. I show you where to find it in yourself.) I know that for the last fifteen years I have been exploring the idea that the more we want to heal the world around us, the more deeply we will need to go into *the as-yet-unreleased energies of the heart*. One way of expressing the intense dynamics of this might be to say that if you want to save a million endangered species, you may need to go a million times deeper into the sources of love and energy hidden within you.

Sawan Singh Maharaj, circa 1940

Here are some of my hunches about what is going on. In general, people seem to mobilize their physical and emotional resources IN PROPORTION to whatever challenges come along. Your muscles develop in proportion to the weights you lift every day. Your response to one stray ant wandering across your kitchen counter would be small in comparison to the response you would have if you saw a house on fire across the street. As the challenges of eco-politics get bigger and bigger, I think people will struggle to mobilize deeper and deeper levels of inner resources, although not necessarily in orderly ways.

For example, contemplating the need to protect all the life of the future from today's nuclear waste sets the psychological stage for a person to become a deeply energized mystic, but also to go mad or commit suicide (several of my friends have done so). In the past such world-saving challenges were very theoretical and I don't know how seriously anyone actually took them. But today's needs to protect life are very concrete and much easier to understand.

Thus, I am thinking that a whole new kind of ecstatic, green, mysticism may emerge from our present crisis. Without realizing it, millions of people, you and I included, have begun doing very intensive Bodhisattva mental exercises. **An infinite demand sets the stage for an infinite response.** We may all suddenly become telepathic, or begin appearing in one another's dreams. Who knows? The shared Darshan experience suggests to me a channel to guide the arrival (or even the eruption) of some new energy.

Prayers of Evolutionary Darshan

As I look into your eyes,
I open my life that I may be a window
through which infinite blessings come to you,
and to everyone, and to everything.

As I look into your eyes,
I open my life to receive the blessings
of the Divine Presence, in you and through you,
and through everyone, and through everything.

May every heart be a window
through which new blessings pour into the world
starting with my heart and yours.

Ever Widening Glimpses of Darshan

Great Bodhisattva – Ajanta Caves

Gray Wolf

Paramahansa Yogananda

Anadamayi Ma

The Fourteenth Dalai Lama

Hazrat Inayat Khan, revered Sufi master

EPILOGUE:

A PRAYER OF SAINT FRANCIS OF THE ALLEGORIAN GALAXY

New Stars Being Formed

Infinitely beautiful Mother Universe
make each of our hearts a fractal instance
of your endless awareness, love, understanding and vitality
woven together, inside of us, between us and among all life forms
into the braid of eternal life.

Where there is injury, across the countless stars,
may we embody such radiant mercy
as to awaken the forgiveness that sleeps in all.

Where there is absent-hearted-ness
and absent-minded-ness
among the 2-leggeds and 7-leggeds
may we embody a fully present compassion
that awakens the compassion sleeping in all.

Where there is deadness masquerading as life
may we embrace life with such gratitude
as to awaken the love of life
sleeping in all creatures.

Where there is sorrow
among the myriad universes
may each of our hearts be a spacetime window
through which your Loving Presence may become
ever more manifest in the visible transmission spectrum.

Wheresoever we shall strive to mend
may we find in the indwelling presence of your Infinite Heart
a kindness deeper and stronger than all conflict.

Wheresoever we shall strive to heal
may we find in the indwelling presence of your Infinite Heart
a beauty deeper and stronger than all wounds.

May we be true to the creative life
you Breathe into us every moment
and may we live in the spiral radiance of your love
forever.

Translated into the Allegorian Hypertext by M345 RuneReader
March 328, 70921 -- www.beamdown.org

I live, teach, write, work, pray and meditate in Eugene, Oregon, and at a whole string of places I have lived along a thousand-mile stretch of Highway 101. My life experiences include having lucid dreams as a young child, a family at war with itself, living through two years of the Cuban Revolution as a teenager in Havana, working in hospitals as a nursing aide, living in a meditation community for several years, building a house by hand on a mountaintop, attempting to practice continuous prayer for nine years, studying psychology, theology, sociology and human development at various universities, learning the art of mental discipline through the craft of computer programming, working as an administrator in social service agencies, and five years writing a workbook on interpersonal communication skills  (that is available free of charge on the web and is now in use around the world).

Having a Jewish mother and a Catholic father who had become a student of Tibetan Buddhism in the years before I was born, provided me with enough questions to keep me journeying for a lifetime. Other significant influences in my life have been Hindu, Sikh, Muslim and Christian mysticism, trees, evolutionary visionaries such as Teilhard de Chardin and Julian Huxley, and the peace and ecology movements of the past forty years.

At this point in many brief author biographies, there is a sentence saying that "X, the author, lives in Y with his wife Z and their three children." I must say, I feel a quiet envy for people who have had long nurturing partnerships with one partner. In my case, my understanding of life has been deeply influenced by the four women with whom I have been partners over the course of my life; for my part of the partnering, not as nurturingly, or wisely or engagingly or gracefully or compassionately as I would have liked. Any summary of my life would be plain false without acknowledging how we labored together to be born as persons. They have been my teachers, and from them I have come to understand that the bond between marriage partners is a fractal of life. The virtues we struggle toward in close relationships, patience, kindness, honesty, gratitude, forgiveness, attentiveness, are the very same virtues that life is trying to teach us all the time, in every circumstance! Some of us, I have to confess, learn these intimate virtues much more slowly than others.

I invite you to share in how I have explored these themes in several different contexts. You can find more of my writing at www.karunabooks.net and also at the other sites I design and write for: www.turntowardlife.org, www.liberationtheology.org and www.nonukes.org. I welcome correspondence about the themes explored in all the above websites. Please feel free to write to me at rivers@newconversations.net.

This painting by Vicky Brago-Mitchell represents to me the amazing variety of experiences I have had in the course of my life, experiences that prompted me to write this book.

Journeys   Fractal painting by Vicky Brago-Mitchell